THE STORY OF MICHAEL'S MUSEUM
A CURIOUS COLLECTION OF TINY TREASURES

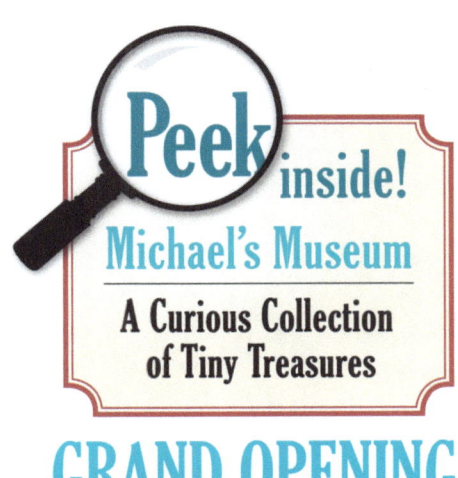

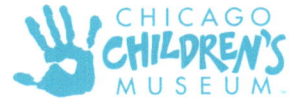

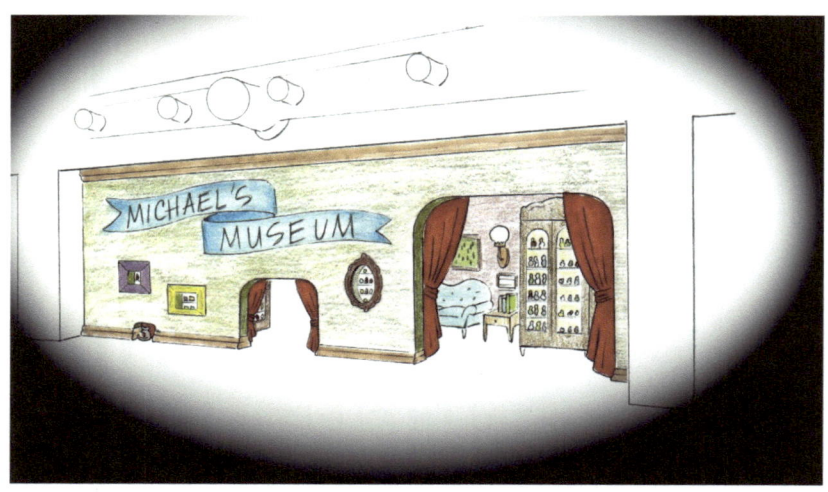

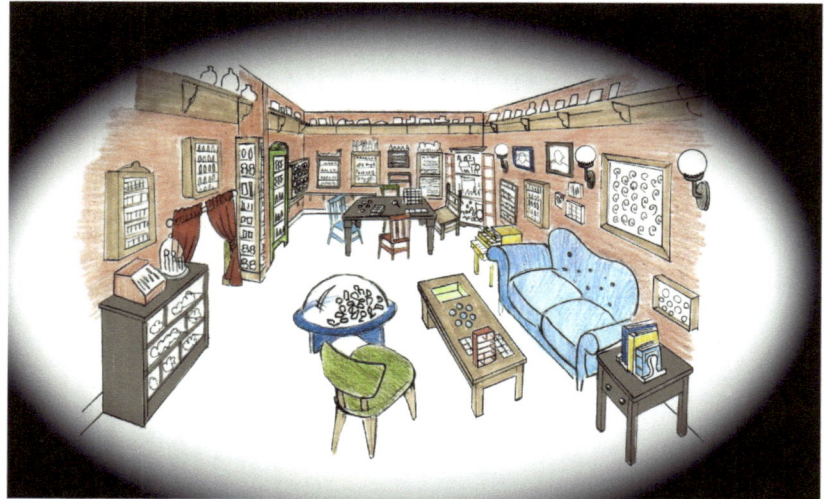

Michael's Museum Souvenir Post Cards

THE STORY OF MICHAEL'S MUSEUM
A CURIOUS COLLECTION OF TINY TREASURES

By: Michael A. Horvich

Written December 2011
Revised October 2020

First Printing 2011

ISBN 9 781716 543418

Michael A. Horvich, Creativity - Publishers
807 Davis Street Suite 415
Evanston, Illinois 60201

www.horvich.com

Dedication

To Children of All Ages
Young Children
Older Children
Grown Up Children
Elderly Children

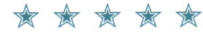

"Step Right Up
Be Amazed, Be Amused, Be Astounded
Feel the Magic, Experience the Joy"

Table of Contents

Sub-Title Page iii
Logo for Michael's Museum iii
Logo for Chicago Children's Museum iii
Children's Museum Post Cards iv
Title Page v
Dedication vii
Table of Contents ix
The Museum Photograph x
The Story of Michael's Museum 1
Exhibit Entrances Protographs 2
Sharing the Joy 3
A Collector is Born 3
The First Exhibit 4
A Bedroom Full of Treasures 5
Growing Up 6
My House, My Museum 6
Treasured Visitors 7
A New Home at Chicago Children's Museum 8
On the Move 9
Sketch by Jenny Schrider, Exhibit Designer 10
Enjoy Your Visit 11
Always Collecting 12
About Michael 13
Collections Photographs 14
Fun Information by the Dozens About Collecting 15
Exhibit Photographs 16

A Dozen Important Things to Remember 17
A Dozen Curious Quotes from the Curator 18
A Dozen Collecting Tips 19
A Dozen Place to Find Collections 20
A Dozen Ways to Display Collections 20
A Dozen Things to Do with Collections 21
A Dozen On-Line Activities 22
A Dozen Things You Would Like to Collect 23
A Dozen Things You Do Collect 24
Tiny Treasure Photos Shown With a Penny For Scale 25
Credits and Thanks 26

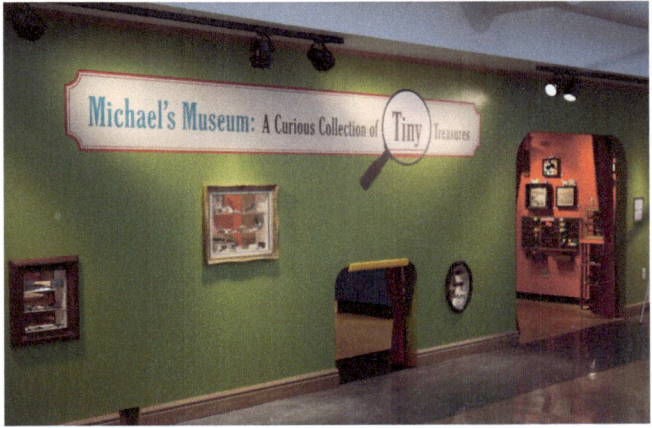

Michael's Museum: A Curious Collection of Tiny Treasures,
a permanent exhibit at Chicago Children's Museum
on Navy Pier since Friday, May 13, 2011

THE STORY OF MICHAEL'S MUSEUM
A CURIOUS COLLECTION OF TINY TREASURES

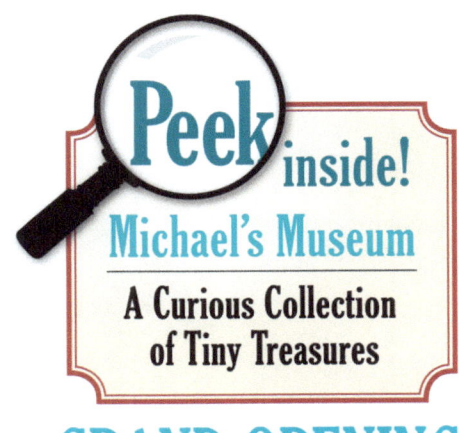

GRAND OPENING

It's the biggest (and tiniest) fun yet—
explore more than 100 enchanting collections!

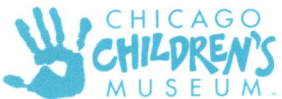

ChicagoChildrensMuseum.org

The Entrances at Michael's Museum

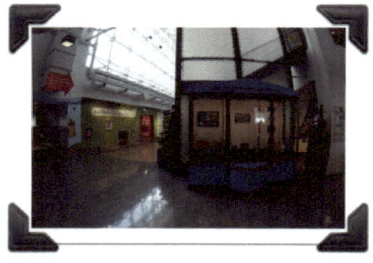

**The Exhibit Entrance
Just Off The Great Hall**

**The Larger Entrance
Probably for Older Visitors**

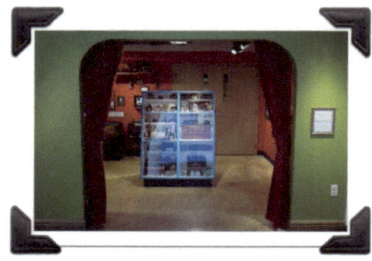

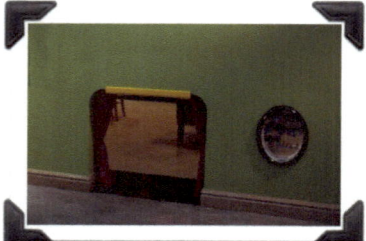

**The Smaller Entrance
Probably for Younger Visitors**

**The Museum Mouse Entrance
robably for the Museum Mouse**

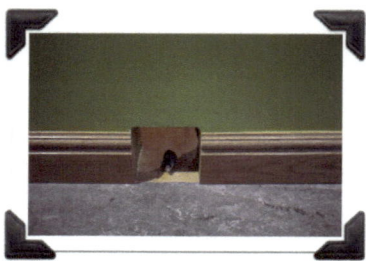

SHARING THE JOY

If I had to sum up why Michael's Museum is so important to me, I would say because it's a way of preserving my youth and "re-parenting" myself. It allows me to remove the pain and confusion of growing up while glorifying and preserving the positive aspects of my youth. Exhibiting my collections allows me to share my joy of life with others.

★ ★

A Collector Is Born

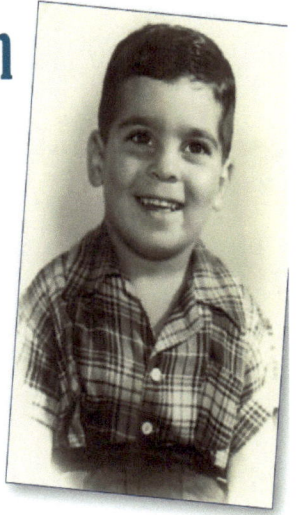

I guess I've been collecting my entire life. As a little boy in the 1950s, I remember filling my pockets with various treasures. None of them were alive—like frogs or such—just small bits and pieces of things that caught my fancy. I remember sitting on the stairs in the hallway outside of a school friend's second floor apartment. We were maybe six or seven years old. He had a cigar box filled with "sparkly things" that his mother had given him. There were bits of broken jewelry, loose sequins, rhinestones, pearls, and silver and gold chains. I remember thinking this was the most wonderful thing I had ever seen. To this day, I can close my eyes and see and feel those things.

★ ★

The First Exhibit

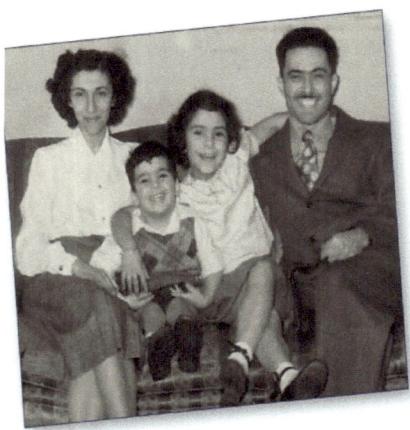

My family lived in Chicago near the corner of Ainslie and Broadway until I was nine years old. Yarnell Chevrolet was just around the corner. I used to set up a lemonade stand and sell drinks for 2¢ to the mechanics who worked there. The stand was a wooden orange crate placed on its side and covered with a tablecloth.

One day, instead of setting up my lemonade stand as usual, I created a "Museum Installation." I used the orange crate and the tablecloth and arranged several "First Place Award" pins I had purchased at the dime store. I set out a display of my favorite things, sat on a stool behind the display, and acted as curator as people walked by.

CURATOR:
the person in charge of a museum or collection

A Bedroom Full of Treasures

When I was nine years old, we moved to Kedzie Avenue in Chicago, and I had my own bedroom. I decorated my bulletin board with rows of rulers suspended from tacked-on string, and arranged my treasures neatly on each ruler. I displayed my metal cars on the windowsill, along with small, "to scale" traffic signs.

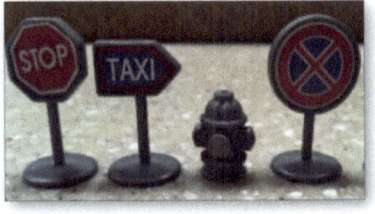

★ ★

Growing Up

My teenage years are a blur. I guess I did the things that teenagers and young adults usually do. I graduated high school, went to college, and began teaching elementary school. I completed my advanced degree and began teaching at the graduate level. I grew up but I never left the "little boy" inside me behind.

As an adult, I was (and still am) always on the lookout for small, magical, interesting, romantic, and/or unique items in neighborhood stores, antique shops, or while traveling. My collection grew and grew.

★ ★

My House, My Museum

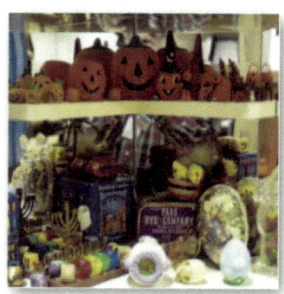

By the 1980s, my collection became a "collection of collections." They were scattered throughout the house until my life partner, Gregory, and I moved into a loft building and he suggested the third floor guestroom be devoted to housing my collections. **Michael's Museum** was born. We hung glass cases on the walls, installed dozens of shelves and bookcases, and added a "curator's desk." During the next five years, my considerable collections doubled in size.

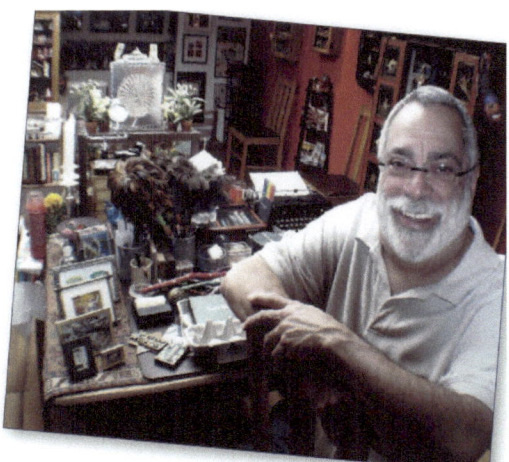

★ ★

Treasured Visitors

Countless friends, friends of friends, neighbors, and family visited Michael's Museum when it was in my home. I delighted in their reactions as an item or collection evoked

Everyone Collects
Even if you don't collect "tiny treasures," you might collect recipes, books, clothes, photographs, ideas, thoughts, experiences…

a childhood memory or reminded them of an item a parent or grandparent had once displayed with love. Sometimes visitors remembered a similar item buried in a drawer at home and promised to unearth it to admire once more.

After new visitors had spent some time playing in the museum, I invited them to select a small item from a treasure box to take home. I loved watching the excitement glitter in their eyes as they went through the box to find the perfect memento. The adults usually took longer to pick one item than the kids did. The museum brought out the "kid" in the adults.

★ ★

A New Home at Chicago Children's Museum

In more recent years, I began to dream of donating Michael's Museum, in its entirety, to an established museum. Even though I collect tiny treasures, I believe "life is meant to be lived big." In a more public place, more people could share and enjoy the wonder and magic of Michael's Museum. I was overjoyed when, in 2007, Chicago Children's Museum (CCM) offered Michael's Museum a permanent home.

On the Move

As you might imagine, moving thousands of tiny treasures was a monumental task.

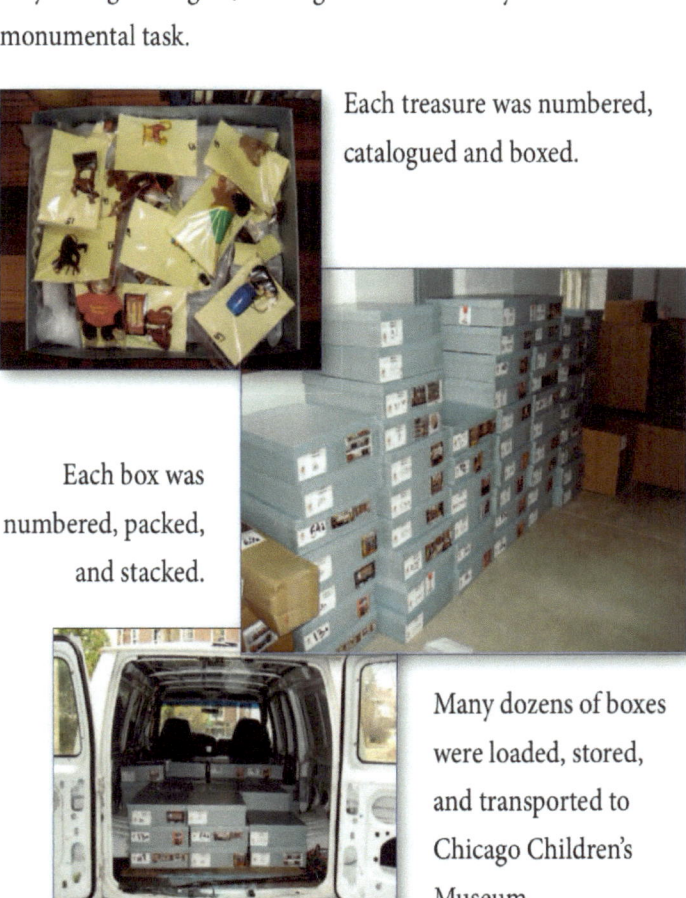

Each treasure was numbered, catalogued and boxed.

Each box was numbered, packed, and stacked.

Many dozens of boxes were loaded, stored, and transported to Chicago Children's Museum.

After a few years in storage, and much planning and installing, Michael's Museum opened at CCM on May 13, 2011!

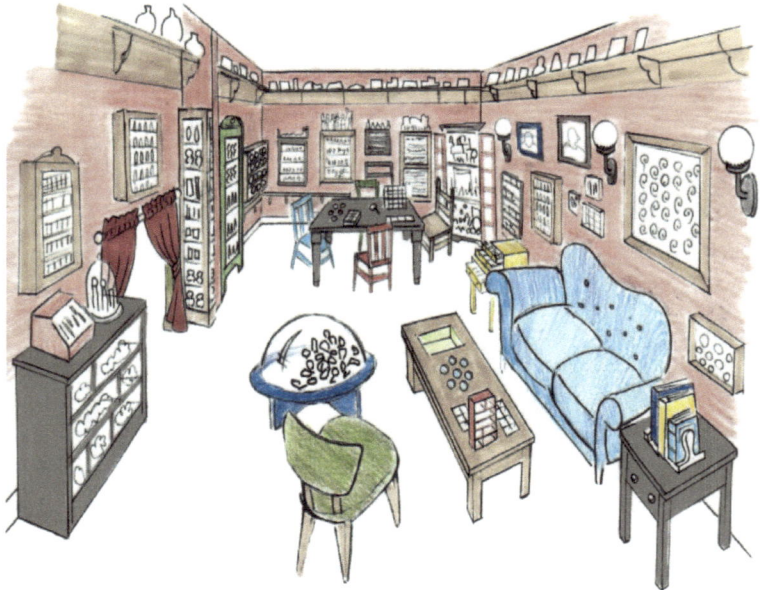

Sketch by designer Jenny Schrider, Fall 2010

Why Collect?
- Collecting helps us learn about and make sense of the world in an organized—or possibly unorganized—way.
- Displaying collections enables us to share ourselves with others.
- Collecting is a way to learn a lot about interesting things—and even become an expert about your collection.

Enjoy Your Visit

I am thrilled to have my curious collections be part of the world-class Chicago Children's Musuem—to have hundreds of thousands of visitors enjoy the hundreds of thousands of tiny treasures displayed here. I hope you feel the magic and experience the joy that I have worked hard to create. I hope something of mine triggers a memory for you, inspiring you to share a story with loved ones and start a collection of your own.

I hope that you will tell everyone you know about your visit to Michael's Museum at Chicago Children's Museum.

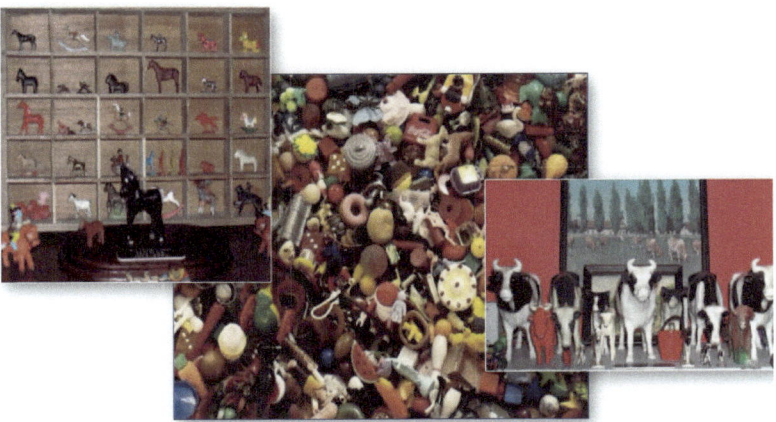

ALWAYS COLLECTING

The Culture of Collecting

When I visit other museums, I am especially drawn to the small things that represent past cultures. To me, these small items are as significant a representation of achievements, beliefs, and day-to-day living as life-size objects.

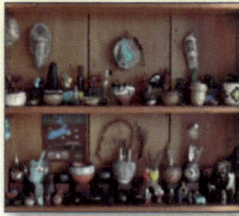

Perhaps the small objects were carried around in a pocket—or perhaps they were used as toys to instruct children, or as part of a religious ceremony.

Gently Loved

I adore items that begin to lose their features. Finding a small statue of a man whose face is rubbed almost smooth makes me happy, as does a worn-out Buddha or a greatly-used child's toy block.

Magic in Numbers

I find that there is magic in numbers, and if I can collect many of the same item, I do. Just as wonderful is having two items that are identical except in size. If I can collect the same object in threes, I am happy. If I can get one of each color—especially all the colors of the rainbow—I am overjoyed.

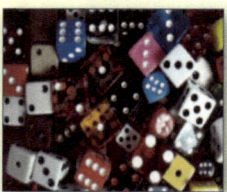

About Michael

EDUCATION:
- Bachelor's Degree from University of Illinois, Champaign/Urbana in Liberal Arts and Sciences, Major in Education/Psychology.
- Master's Degree from National Louis University, Evanston, Illinois, in Gifted Education.
- Advanced Certificate from The University of Illinois, Champaign/Urbana, in Educational Supervision and Administration.

EDUCATOR:
- Children's Program Assistant - Illinois Department of Mental Health
- Teacher - HEED School - Childhood Autism
- Director - MARC Day Camp - Disabled Children
- Teacher - AHRC School - Developmentally Disabled Children
- Substitute Teacher - Champaign Schools
- Teacher - Northbrook Schools, 4th and 5th grade
- Teacher - Glenview Schools, Jr. High Spanish
- Director of Gifted Education - Glenview School District 34
- Founding member/secretary - Illinois Association for Gifted Children
- Adjunct Faculty - National Louis University
- Workshop Presenter - State of Illinois Gifted Education Conferences
- Teacher - State Education Department
- Published Author

AWARDS:
- Two-time State of Illinois Gifted Education Fellowship Award
- Chicago Council on Fine Arts for "Maybe-the-Clown and His Back Pocket Review"
- The Ragdale Foundation's Competitive Application Residency in Creative Non-Fiction writing

ARTS:
- Jane Adams Hull House - Book Binder/Artist Show
- Casa Norte Chicago - Photography and Jewelry Show
- Lyric Opera of Chicago - Supernumerary (Acting Extra)
- Sherman Plaza Art Show - Photography and Jewelry
- In the Table Gallery - Collections Installation
- Chicago Children's Museum - Michael's Museum, Curator

Collections Photographs

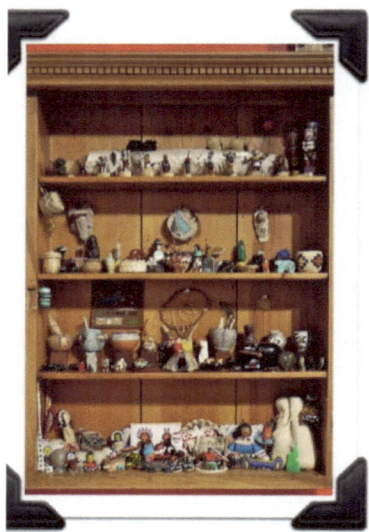
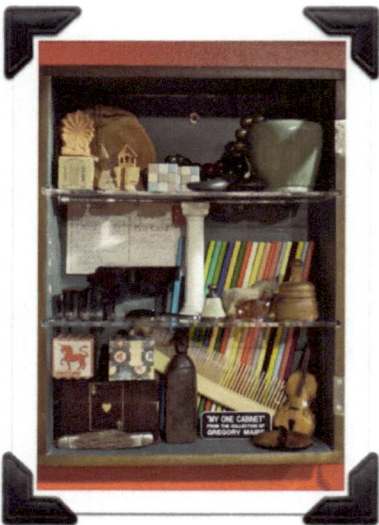
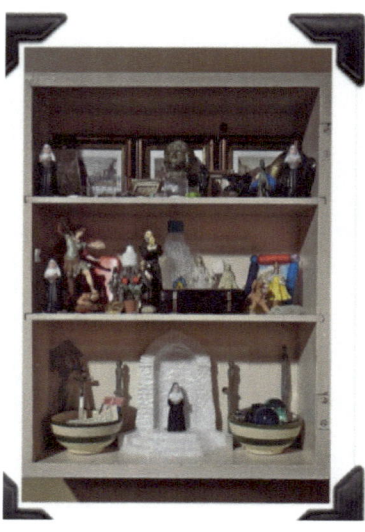
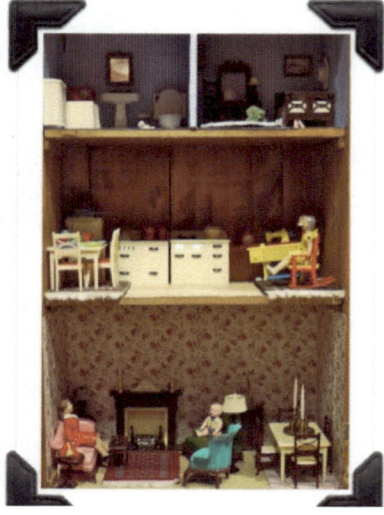

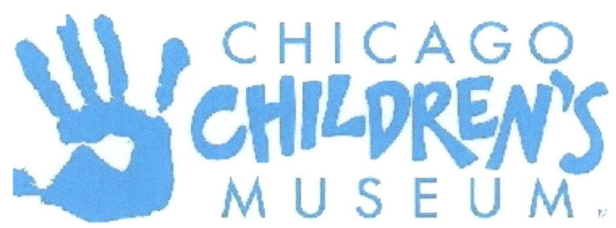

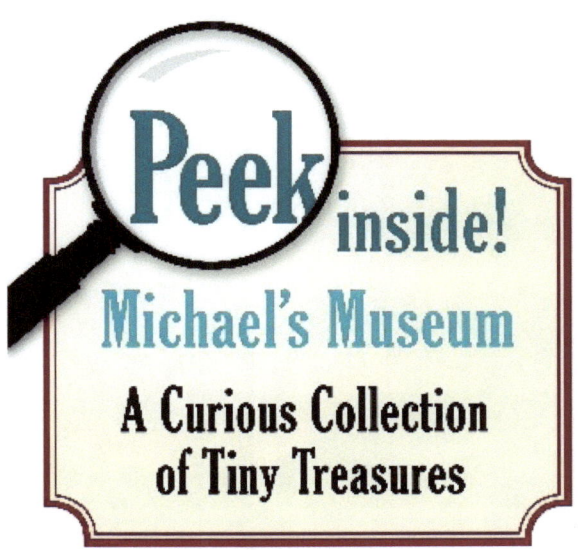

Fun Information By the Dozens About Collecting

Exhibit Photographs

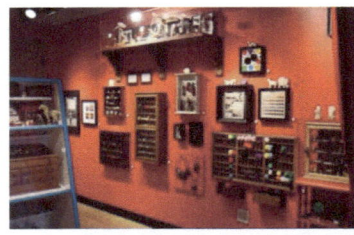
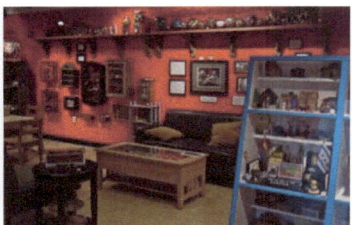
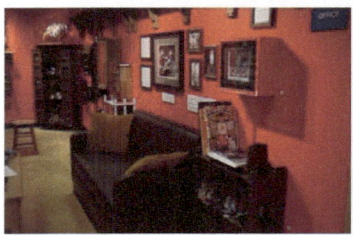
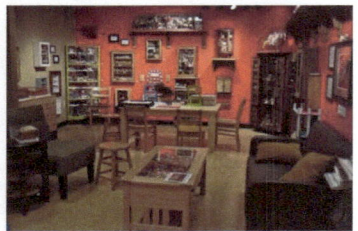
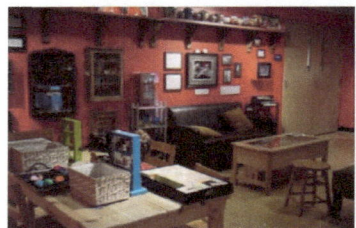
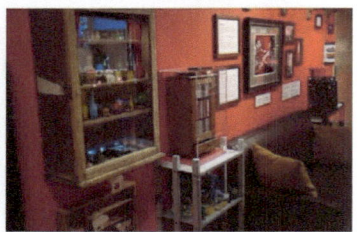
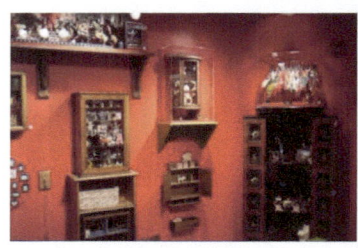
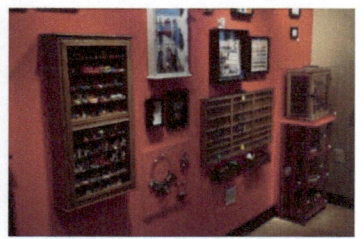
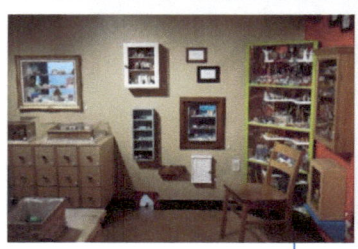
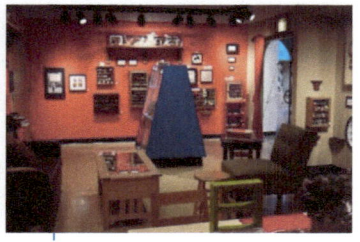

A Dozen Important Things to Remember About Collections

1. A collection can consist of two or more items.

2. Some collections have hundreds of pieces, some only a few.

3. If you find duplicates of items you collect, collect them too!

4. There is magic in repetition.

5. Display of collections is important.

6. Just keeping collections in your dresser is important also.

7. Boxes filled with "stuff" are wonderful.

8. Carrying "stuff" in a pocket is fun.

9. Giving an item to a friend now and then is nice to do.

10. Always be on the lookout for interesting things to collect.

11. Items for your collection can be purchased, received as a gift, found outside, or can be created by you or someone you know.

12. Collections can be anything you want them to be.

A Dozen Quotes From the Curator

1. Life is the art of collecting.
2. Go into a shop without anything specific in mind and let a small item select you.
3. The pocket is a wonderful treasure chest.
4. It only takes two items to make a collection.
5. Michael's Museum, an interpretation of the beauty, magic, and essence of life reduced to something that can be held in your hand.
6. Collections can be fun when carefully displayed or when tossed into a cigar box.
7. The exact number of items in the Michael's Museum is unknown, and I'm keeping it that way.
8. Be amazed, be amused, be astounded. Feel the magic, experience the joy.
9. Michael's Museum is a way of preserving the memories and fantasies of childhood.
10. In collecting you can earn again or for the first time, the child's eye of discovery.
11. Michael's Museum is more than just miniatures: it is trinkets, little things, tiny curiosities, minuscule discoveries, small oddities, artifacts, teensy items.
12. While I love little things, I love to think, dream, and live big.

A Dozen Tips on Collecting

1. We all collect! If not tiny treasures, then ideas, memories, photographs, books, music, jewelry, experiences, etc.
2. Parents need to encourage children to collect.
3. There is always time to collect. Don't think collecting is just for the young!
4. Collections need not be troublesome. Some of the same rules for appropriate behavior apply to collecting: "keep your room neat," "don't leave things all over the house," "Only 3 types for now!"
5. Inexpensive display cabinets can be purchased to display collections. The glass front lets you see the items while keeping them mostly dust free.
6. Collecting need not cost a lot of money and can consist of things received, given, found, foraged, created as well as purchased.
7. Sometimes collections fall out of favor. After discussing the change of heart; collections can be stored for possible use, given away, sold at garage sales.
8. Never get rid of your child's collection without first discussing it with him or her.
9. Collections of boxes filled with stuff can be fun.
10. Collecting can be a learning experience.
11. Any age child can collect. Careful of choking.
12. Collections can be anything you want them to be!

A Dozen Places to Find Collections

1. In your home.
2. In the home of friends or family. (With permission!)
3. Outside your home.
4. Outside in your neighborhood.
5. Outside in the neighborhoods of friends or family.
6. On the street. (Stay with adults. Be careful of cars!)
7. At the park or at the beach.
8. At the grocery store.
9. At an antique shop.
10. At the dollar store.
11. At garage sales and flea markets.
12. On vacation.

A Dozen Ways to Show Collections

1. In a cigar box.
2. In an egg carton.
3. On a shelf.
4. On a window sill.
5. On your desk.
6. On a table.
7. In a glass front cabinet.
8. In a deep picture frame.
9. Hanging from the ceiling.
10. On the kitchen counter ledge.
11. Push pinned to a bulletin board.
12. In a bowl or dish or any container.

A Dozen Things to Do With Your Collections

1. First of all, you have to collect your collection or collect a collection of collections.
2. Arrange your collections in a way that shows them off beautifully.
3. Stash your collections in a box and hide it in a drawer.
4. Now and then, dump your collections on a table and look through them.
5. Learn about HOW, WHERE, WHEN, WHY the items in your collections were made.
6. Read about your collections in books or do a Google search.
7. Write true stories about your collections.
8. Make up stories about your collections.
9. Make a list of the items in your collections with a brief description of each one.
10. Trade your collections with friends or family.
11. Sort, categorize, and re-sort the items in your collections.
12. Start new collections.

A Dozen On-Line Activities

1. Find out more about your collections on Google.
2. Search Google for "Miniatures."
3. Chicago Children's Museum.: http:// www.chicagochildrens-museum.org
4. Michael's Museum BLOG: http://michaelcollects.blogspot.com
5. Visit Chicago Children's Museum on facebook.
6. Visit Michael's Museum on facebook.
7. Upload picture of your collections (with you next to them if you choose) on CCM and MM facebook
8. Miniature Thorne Rooms at the Art Institute: http:// www.artic.edu/aic/collections/artwork/category/15
9. Miniature Colleen Moore's Fairy Castle, Chicago Museum of Science & Industry: http://www.msichicago.org/whats-here/exhibits/fairycastle/
10. U-Tube for Willard Wiggins' miniature carvings in the eye of a needle: http://www.youtube.com/watch?v=oKhvREI5BUQ
11. Miniatur Wunderland's largest miniature model railway in the world: http://www.youtube.com/watch?v=PN_oDdGmKyA
12. "Dot," The world's smallest stop-motion animation character:http://www.youtube.com/watch?v=CD7eagLl5c4&feature=youtube_gdata_player

Name or Clip Pictures of 12 Things You Would Like to Collect

1.

2.

3.

4.

5.

6.

7.

8.

9.

10.

11.

12.

Name or Draw 12 Pictures of Things You Do Collect

1.

2.

3.

4.

5.

6.

7.

8.

9.

10.

11.

12.

TINY TREASURES
Shown with penny for scale

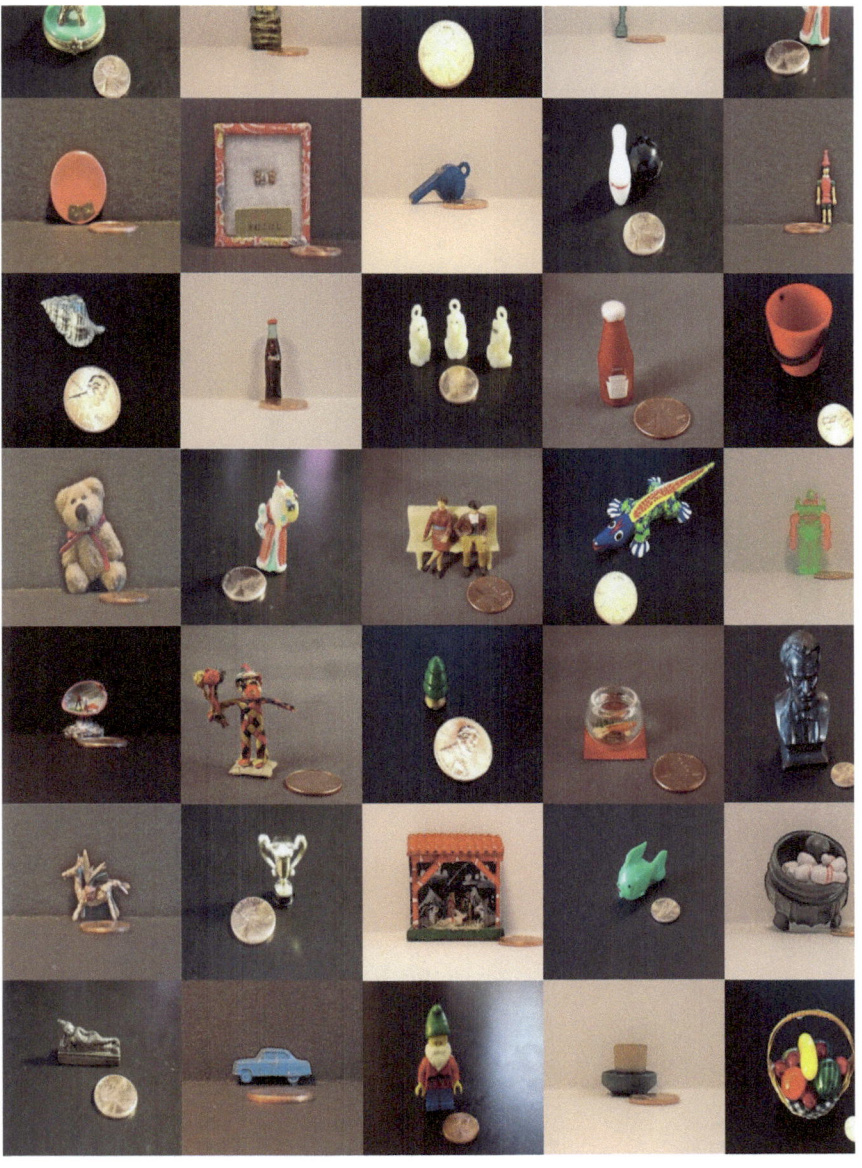

Michael's Museum
A Curious Collection of Tiny Treasures

Is like a tree of wisdom where learning takes place!

Curiosities,
Trinkets, Artifacts
Miniatures, Findings,
Littles, Smalls, Tinys
Discoveries & Miniatures
A collection of 105 collections
An amazing folk art installation
A look at life as the art of collecting
Earning again the child's eye of discovery
Intergenerational interaction, sharing, and learning
Activities, discussions, workshops, and other activities
Holding the past and present while looking to the future
Celebrating individual differences for kids, families, and teachers
An interpretation of the beauty in life reduced to be held in one hand
Experiencing, wondering, musing, questioning, sharing, storytelling
and much more

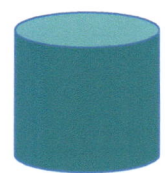

CREDITS & THANKS
The Michael's Museum Creative Team

Jennifer Farrington – CEO & President
Louise Belmont Skinner – VP of Exhibits
Katie Slivovsky – Exhibit Developer
Michele Boglio – Project Manager
Natalie Bortoli – Education Developer
Jenny Schrider – Designer
Benjamin Waite – Visitor Advocate
Mark Frank – Head Preparator
Patrick Downs – Assistant Preparator
Rick Cassettari – Support Preparator
Peter Williams – Associate VP of Exhibit & Building Operations
Jennifer Joyce – VP of Marketing
Natalie Kreiger – Director of Public Relations
Stephanie Lieber – VP of Individual Giving
Jon Resh – Artistic Director
Ellen Sanderson – Graphics Designer
Brett Taylor – Special Projects Coordinator President Office
Jasmine Raehl – Gift Shop Manager
And Michael A. Horvich – Donor, Curator, Collections Expert

SPECIAL THANKS TO

Mom, Dad, Gregory Maire, Marla Weismantel, Amethel Parel-Sewell, Barbara Mahany, Chris Walker, Barbara Unikel, Jenny Schrider, Sheila Scullin, and The Museum Mouse

MICHAEL'S BIOGRAPHY

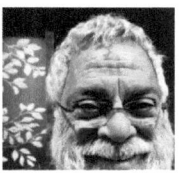

Michael is an educator, speaker, story-teller, writer, poet, photographer, blogger, artist, jeweler, book binder, lecturer, actor, opera supernumerary, collector, museum curator, flea circus ring master, and was a Dementia/Alzheimer's caregiver partner for his life partner Gregory Maire (RIP 2015.)

He won two Fellowships in Gifted Education from the State of Illinois, a Performing Arts Grant from the City of Chicago, and a two-week Competitive Application Residency in creative non-fiction writing at The Ragdale Foundation in Lake Forest, Illinois.

Michael's Museum: A Curious Collection of Tiny Treasures, a folk art collection of over 105 collections of Tiny Treasures was installed as a permanent exhibit at The Chicago Children's Museum on Navy Pier in May, 2011.

He and his life partner Gregory Maire (RIP 2015) are the subject of ALZHEIMER'S: A Love Story, which has been accepted locally, nationally, and internationally by 90+ film festivals and has won 35+ awards including both the Best Short Film and Best LGBTQ Film at the Cannes American Pavilion Emerging Filmmakers Showcase.

He has appeared on stage as a Supernumerary, an acting extra, at Lyric Opera of Chicago in 20 operas over a period of 13 years.

Michael has made presentations on "Living Well with Alzheimer's," "The Dimensions of Grief and Love With Alzheimer's," and "The Importance of Art in Dementia Care," at a number of conferences and venues including: The North Shore University Health Care System Annual Symposium, The Evanston Art Center, The Alzheimer's Disease International Conference, and as opening key note speaker and also facilitator of an hour break-out session on Grief for the MN/MD Chapter of the Alzheimer's Association's "Meeting of the Minds" conference in conjunction with The Mayo Clinic of Rochester, MN.

He is currently working on his memoirs: GYROSCOPE: An Alzheimer's Love Story; a musical: ALZHEIMER'S: The Musical; an opera: ALZHEIMER'S: The Opera; a play: ALZHEIMER'S: The Dialogues; and at establishing a second museum of miniatures, a traveling museum/art exhibit called The Small.

Michael is 75 years old and lives in Evanston with his cats Emma and Gigi, and the fond memories of his love, Gregory.

• • • • •

Michael has been published in a number of educational journals. He has published two poetry books: Sit With Me A While and Sit With Me A While Longer. Also he has written: The Story of Michael's Museum, and Counting Down the Yardstick: A Reincarnation Memoir. All are available at:

www.lulu.com, www.amazon.com,
and www.barnesandnobel.com

Follow Michael on his website: www.horvich.com

www.ingramcontent.com/pod-product-compliance
Lightning Source LLC
Chambersburg PA
CBHW040251220526
45473CB00001B/448